To every child that has left a handprint on my
heart, this book is for you.

A Hand On Your Heart

Written by Lisa Shetler

Illustrated by Danika Runyan

A tricky thing happened and
inside it hurt.

Like a wave growing larger,
Swallowing up all your words.

To a friend you would say:
I'm here and I care.

But Inside
Your Mind,
A Bully
Lives There.

It says: stop being silly, stop crying, you sook!

And that's why, together, we're reading this book.

Gently and softly, whisper with me: It's hard, and I see you. We can sit and just be.

I feel Sad...

I'm
here

With your hands on
your heart,

Or your cheeks, or
your knees...

Wrap yourself up in kindness
and give a soft squeeze.

Hurt feelings are hard
whether you're little or big.

Showing kindness both ways can help us forgive.

So, next time you're hurting, remember that you

are your own caring friend,
you know what to do.

Be kind to your mind and your heart and your toes.

Notice your feelings, then watch as they go.

About the Author

Lisa is a clinical psychologist and self-compassion teacher with over a decade of experience working in child and adolescent mental health. She is the director of two psychology practices and is an internationally recognised teacher and trainer of self-compassion for children and teens. Lisa and her husband are also foster carers and have provided care for children from birth through the adolescent years, witnessing first hand the devastating impact of trauma and abuse on young children and the need for resources that support their development.

Of all the therapeutic tools and interventions at her disposal, Lisa finds that self-compassion continues to be one of the most valuable and vital skills to help alleviate suffering, improve wellbeing and prevent the development of mental illness. It is Lisa's hope that this book provides an introduction to the teachings of self-compassion for young children and the adults around them so that from the earliest possible age, children grow up with a supportive and kind inner voice.

A guide on self Compassion for kids

As a clinical psychologist and self-compassion teacher who specialises in working with children and young people, I have seen first hand the detrimental impact of children not having the tools and resources to manage challenging situations and emotions. Even very young children can internalise a harsh and self-critical voice that amplifies feelings of guilt and shame, and gives rise to the ever-pervasive worry of 'I'm not good enough'. The consequences of this on a young person's mental health can be extreme, leading to anxiety, perfectionism, depression and harmful ways of coping.

Self-compassion has been shown to act as a powerful shield against self-criticism and the mental health challenges that can arise from it. It lays the critical foundation for emotional well-being, empathy, resilience and children's confidence in their ability to cope. Children who learn how to befriend themselves during tough times are more likely to take greater responsibility for their actions, have improved relationships with others, be able to motivate themselves with kindness, and experience reduced risk of mental illness.

As caregivers, educators and therapists working with kids, you have the immense privilege and responsibility of teaching and modelling how mindfulness, kindness and connection to others (the three components of self-compassion) can become superpowers that help us thrive.

In the pages that follow you will find extended self-compassion teachings and practices that are referred to in the story. I invite you to practise these yourself and share them with the children in your life so that they may learn how to be their own caring friend in times of need.

How would I treat a friend?

It's true that most people are far more willing to show care and kindness to others as compared to themselves; children are much the same. When asked how they might respond to a friend who had made a mistake, broken something, or not done well, most children will intuitively offer words of support like: "it's ok", "you can try again", "I can help you", or offer a kind gesture such as a hug or offering to get help. Yet, when we hear the way children talk to themselves in these same situations, they are often overly critical, self-blaming and pessimistic: "what's wrong with me", "I can't do it", "I'm a bad kid", "crying is weak".

One of the simplest ways to begin introducing self-compassion to children is to ask them what they would say to a close friend or relative if they were in this situation. This helps to elicit the kind voice that is already inherent within the child. We can then curiously wonder together what it might be like if the child offered themselves that same kindness. In this way we are inviting the child to include themselves in the circle of people that are deserving of care and kindness when they are hurting, rather than seeing themselves as separate or unworthy of love and kindness.

Here's an example of how that conversation might go:

Situation: child loses a race and is feeling upset and frustrated.

Adult: Hey kiddo, I saw you really trying your best out there. How do you feel?

Child: I hate running, I'm the worst one. I'm never doing it again.

Adult: It was really challenging and it looks like you're disappointed.

Child: I'm never going to win a race.

Adult: It's hard when things don't work out the way we want them to. I wonder what you would say to your friend if they had come last today?

Child: I would tell them, it's ok and they can try again next time.

Adult: And what if they were really upset?

Child: I'd give them a hug.

Adult: I wonder what it would be like if you told yourself something like that? That you did your best today and you can try again next time.

Child: That would feel better.

Adult: Would you like a hug, or like to try giving yourself one?

Notice, Name, Allow

We all know what happens when we bottle up our feelings. It may seem like a solution in the short term, but over time they build up, begin bubbling to the surface, and eventually burst out – just like a soft drink bottle that has been shaken over and over. Using the skills of mindfulness (paying attention to what is happening in the present moment with curiosity) we can support kids to become aware of their emotions and the body sensations that visit along with them. This is one of the first steps in helping children manage their feelings and regulate their bodies.

We can invite kids to tune in and get curious about what they notice in their body, then give the feeling a name and allow it to be there without trying to push it away or get rid of it. This helps to contain the emotional experience, normalise that emotions are a healthy part of life, and increases the child's self-awareness and ability to communicate about their inner experiences. The result is that the emotion is likely to move on far more quickly and easily than when we struggle against it and try to push it away.

With younger children, you may need to offer your observations and provide labels for their emotions. For example: "I can see you want to hide. I wonder if you're feeling nervous?" or, "your face has gotten very red. I can see you're really angry about this".

When we support kids to notice what is happening in their body, name the emotion and allow that experience to be what it is, we are helping them to learn that they and their emotions are OK, that we are willing and able to stay with them and support them through it, and that eventually the feelings resolve on their own. A great way of helping kids picture this is to think of how waves rise and fall in the ocean. They build up to a peak, crash and then disappear. Riding out emotions is a bit like riding over the waves of life.

Comforting Gestures

"Mama, can you kiss it better?" Most parents know the almost magical healing power of a kiss or a cuddle when a kiddo is hurt. We hold a child's hand to communicate presence and safety, we offer a hug to show love and care, we rub their backs when they are sick, we wrap them, rock them and pat them to soothe them from birth. Physical gestures of comfort soothe the body and help settle the mind. Research has shown that giving yourself a hug can generate similar positive biological changes as receiving a hug from someone else.

Some common compassionate gestures that you can teach your child include:

Placing one or both hands over their heart. Inviting them to notice the gentle pressure of their hands on their chest and feel their heart beat
Giving themselves a hug by crossing their arms and gently rubbing or squeezing their shoulders or upper arms
Hugging their knees into their chest and curling into a ball
Holding their own hand, either by resting them in their lap, clasping them together or pressing fingertips together
Placing one or both hands on their cheeks in a gentle embrace while they take a slow deep breath
Wrapping themselves up in a blanket or having a cuddle with a soft toy

These small gestures are a physical reminder to show ourselves comfort and kindness when things are hard and can help to keep us grounded in the present moment when emotions are running high.

Modelling self-kindness and forgiveness

More than listening to the words we say, kids are constantly learning by watching what we do. When they see us being hard on ourselves, they are likely to do the same. Conversely, when we model self-acceptance, curiosity and understanding, kids are more likely to emulate this. This can also help to teach kids empathy and understanding towards others, which serve as essential skills for fostering healthy friendships and relationships.

It's a common myth of self-compassion that showing understanding when we make a mistake will lead to a lack of responsibility, 'being too easy on ourselves' or 'letting ourselves off the hook too easily'. In fact, the opposite is true. All available evidence suggests that people who rate higher in self-compassion also are more likely to admit when they have made a mistake, take responsibility for their actions, and achieve higher levels of success in their pursuits due to being able to bounce back from failures and motivate themselves to keep going.

Next time you spill something, break something or things don't go to plan, try narrating out loud what's happened, how you're feeling and what you're going to do to help yourself learn from the mistake and try again. This may feel a little odd at first but the more you practise, the more natural it will feel and your kiddo will get the benefit of learning from your example.